"By Grace, Be Free"

An Inductive Study
in
The Book of Galatians

*"I have been crucified with Christ; it is no longer I who live,
but Christ lives in me; and the life which I now live in the flesh
I live by faith in the Son of God, who loved me and gave Himself for me."
Galatians 2:20*

Published By
Morningstar Christian Chapel
Whittier, California 90603

"By Grace, Be Free"
An Inductive Study in The Book of Galatians
Copyright © 2005 by Morningstar Christian Chapel
Published by Morningstar Christian Chapel
ISBN: 978-0-9729477-5-6

Additional copies of this book are available by contacting:

Morningstar Christian Chapel
Whittier, California 90603
562.943.0297

Introduction to Galatians

The Book of Galatians is most likely the first book Paul ever wrote and it has come to be known as the Magna Carta of spiritual liberty. The message throughout the book is clearly salvation by grace. The church in Galatia had begun their Christian experience by faith, but was now turning again to the works of the Law. Paul boldly declares them "foolish" for such turning back.

AUTHOR:

The author of Galatians is the Apostle Paul. Paul, who was originally known as Saul, was born in Tarsus, a city in southeast Asia Minor not far from Galatia. After vigorously persecuting the Christian church, Paul found himself face to face with Jesus on the road to Damascus (Acts 22). From that moment his life was transformed and he became a bold evangelist traveling much of the known world sharing and teaching Jesus Christ.

TIME OF WRITING:

On Paul's first missionary journey he established four churches in the southern part of the Galatia region. These churches are mentioned in Acts 13-14. Although Galatians does not specifically mention any churches by name, it is well known that Paul ministered personally to these churches. The time of writing is placed at about 50 A.D,

KEY VERSES:

GALATIANS 2:20 & 21 GIVES US AN AWESOME SUMMARY OF PAUL'S LETTER TO THE GALATIANS:

> "I have been crucified with Christ; it is no longer I who live, but Christ lives in me; and the life which I now live in the flesh I live by faith in the Son of God, who loved me and gave Himself for me. "I do not set aside the grace of God; for if righteousness comes through the law, then Christ died in vain."

by Grace, *be* Free

We would do well to add Galatians 5:1 to remind us not to fall into the trap of legalism and works that plagued the Galatian churches as Paul was writing:

Stand fast therefore in the liberty by which Christ has made us free, and do not be entangled again with a yoke of bondage.

BACKGROUND INFORMATION

The difference between the letters to the Corinthians and this one to the Galatians is that the Corinthians had the right doctrine but they were disobedient, whereas, those in Galatia were embracing false doctrine and the false teachers known as Judiazers were trampling the grace of God under foot. "Their false teaching" claimed that the Gentiles had to first become Jews and practice the Law in order to be saved. Paul's message was clear and concise, and it is as important for us today as it was in A.D. 50.

The diligent study of the Letter to the Galatians will set you free to come to Jesus solely on the basis of His grace.

Outline of Galatians

I. Declaring and Defending the Gospel of Grace (1:1 – 2:21)

    A. Paul's call to declare the message of grace

    B. Paul's defense of grace before the church

    C. Paul's defense of grace before Peter

II. Explaining Grace and the Law   (3:1 – 4:31)

    A. Having been set free – why return?

    B. God's Riches at Christ's Expense

    C. The Law as a tutor to bring us to Christ

    D. Living as a Child of Promise

III. Living the Gospel of Grace Daily (5:1 – 6:18)

    A. Stand Fast in Christ's Liberty

    B. Walk in the Spirit

    C. Fruit of the Spirit

    D. Final Words on the Gospel of Grace

by Grace, be Free

Lesson Index

Remember to begin every Bible Study in Prayer.
It is the Holy Spirit that leads us into all truth.

"But the Helper, the Holy Spirit, whom the Father will send in My name, He will teach you all things, and bring to your remembrance all things that I said to you.

(John 14:26, NKJV)

DAY 1 – BEGIN IN PRAYER

1.   Read Galatians 1.

2.   Who is the author? What do you learn about him?

3.   What are the main topics and lessons in Chapter 1?

4.   What warnings, exhortations, or instructions are given?

5.   How will you personally apply these truths to your life today?

6.   Use Galatians 5:1 as a memory verse for this week. Begin working on it today.

DAY 2 – BEGIN IN PRAYER

1.   Read Galatians 2.

2.   What are the main topics and lessons in Chapter 2?

by GRACE, *be* Free

3.　What warnings, exhortations, or instructions are given?

4.　Are there any promises to stand upon?

5.　How will you personally apply these truths to your life today?

6.　Continue to work on your memory verse!

DAY 3 ~ BEGIN IN PRAYER

1.　Read Galatians 3.

2.　What are the main topics and lessons in Chapter 3?

3.　What warnings, exhortations, or instructions are given?

4.　Are there any promises to stand upon?

5.　How will you personally apply these truths to your life today?

6.　Continue to work on your memory verse!

DAY 4 ~ BEGIN IN PRAYER

1. Read Galatians 4.

2. What are the main topics and lessons in Chapter 4?

3. What warnings, exhortations, or instructions are given?

4. Are there any promises to stand upon?

5. How will you personally apply these truths to your life today?

6. Continue to work on your memory verse!

DAY 5 ~ BEGIN IN PRAYER

1. Read Galatians 5.

2. What are the main topics and lessons in Chapter 5?

3. What warnings, exhortations, or instructions are given?

4. Are there any promises to stand upon?

5. How will you personally apply these truths to your life today?

6. Continue to work on your memory verse!

DAY 6 – BEGIN IN PRAYER

1. Read Galatians 6.

2. What are the main topics and lessons in Chapter 6?

3. What warnings, exhortations, or instructions are given?

4. Are there any promises to stand upon?

5. How will you personally apply these truths to your life today?

6. Record your memory verse. (Were you able to do it without looking?)

Your Word I have hidden in my heart, that I might not sin against You!
                              (Psalms 119:11, NKJV)

DAY 1 ~ BEGIN IN PRAYER

1. Read Galatians 1.

2. Re-read Galatians 1:1-9.

3. What do you learn about Paul's calling?

4. How does Paul clearly define the true Gospel?

5. What was the severe issue facing the churches in the region of Galatia that caused Paul to write this letter?

6. Your memory verse for this week is Galatians 1:9. Record it below and begin committing it to memory today.

DAY 2 ~ BEGIN IN PRAYER

1. Read Galatians 1.

2. Re-read Galatians 1:1-2.

3. One way to deny the truthfulness of a message is to deny the authority of the one who delivers the message. Paul had planted these churches in Galatia on his first and second missionary journeys, and now he is sending a letter of correction because they were quickly following after the false teaching of the Judiazers. Compare the introduction of this letter with the introduction of Romans, Philippians, Titus and Philemon. What is different?

_by_ **GRACE,**
_be_ **Free**

Why do you think Paul only uses his title of Apostle in the letter to the Galatians?

4. Use a Dictionary of New Testament Words to learn more about the term *apostle* as it is used in the New Testament.

Read Acts 9:1-22 and record the details of Paul's calling that substantiate his authority as an *apostle* of Jesus Christ.

What further insight into Paul's *apostleship* do you gain from 1Corinthians 15:1-10?

5. Use a Bible Map to locate the churches in the region of Galatia. What are the names of a few of them and what do you learn about Paul's experiences in these cities?

    a. Acts 14:1-25

    b. Acts 16:1-5

6. What specific lesson(s) did you learn from today's study and how will it make a difference in how you live this week?

7. Continue to work on memorizing Galatians 1:9 for this week. Do not neglect this important part of the study.

DAY 3 – BEGIN IN PRAYER

1. Read Galatians 1.

2. Re-read Galatians 1: 3-5.

3. Paul begins his letter with a two-word greeting (v. 3) that is seen at the beginning of many of his writings. What are they and why do you think that Paul so often linked the two together?

    Grace is the source of salvation and it describes our position in Christ Jesus, and **peace** is the practical outcome of this relationship of grace. Without the grace of God operating in our lives, true peace is impossible to obtain. How would you describe and define the grace of God?

    According to Ephesians 2:8, 9, can the grace of God be merited, earned or deserved?

    What do we learn from the following Scriptures about the peace of God?

    a. John 14:27

    b. John 16:33

    c. Romans 5:1, 2

    d. Romans 8:5, 6

4. In the earliest sentences of this letter Paul makes it clear that the true Gospel message is centered on a *Person*, a *price*, and a *purpose*. According to Galatians 1:3-4, Who and what are they?

a. The Person =

b. The price =

c. The purpose =

The Judaizers, who were plaguing the churches in the region of Galatia, were challenging the very heart of the Gospel. In turning back to legalism, these saints had ignored the significance of Christ's death; salvation is not earned through a set of religious rituals and obedience to the Law, it is a gift based on faith in the sacrificial death and resurrection of Jesus Christ, our Savior. The purpose of His coming was that He might deliver us from this evil age. His mission was a rescue mission; His goal was to save us from a doomed world. What do the following Scriptures teach us about this world system we live in, and our relationship to it?

a. John 14:30

b. 2Corinthians 4:3, 4

c. Colossians 1:12-14

d. John 17:15, 16

5. Paul writes that this plan of salvation was *according to the will of our God and Father, to whom be glory forever and ever.* He alone is to be honored for this saving grace found in Jesus Christ. The false teachers in Galatia were not ministering for the glory of Christ, but for their own glory. In our lives, all the glory for His every good work is to be given to our Heavenly Father and our Lord Jesus Christ for His finished work on the cross at Calvary. Record Jude 1:24, 25 and make it your prayer of praise today.

6. What specific lesson(s) did you learn from today's study, and how will it make a difference in how you live this week?

7. Continue to work on memorizing Galatians 1:9.

DAY 4 – BEGIN IN PRAYER

1. Read Galatians 1.

2. Re-read Galatians 1:6-7.

3. Paul *marveled (to be astounded, bewildered, or amazed)*, not that the false teachers could teach such lies, but that the saints would buy into them so quickly. The Galatians were in the process of deserting *Him who called them in the grace of Christ*. They were willfully moving in the wrong direction. What warning is given to the church to put us on guard against false teaching?

   a. Matthew 7:15-20

   b. Colossians 2:8

   c. 2Peter 3:17

4. What is the guaranteed protection given to us that will keep us from falling for false teaching?

   a. 2Peter 3:18

   b. Colossians 1:9, 10

c. 2Timothy 2:15

5. The believers in Galatia were turning away to a *different gospel*, which was really not the Gospel at all. The danger of false teaching is that there is often a large percentage of truth mixed with fatal error. Most of it looks good – but it perverts the truth and the result is false doctrine. The Judaizers were adding the Law to grace. You cannot mix grace and works, because the one excludes the other. Use a Dictionary of New Testament Words to define the following strong words Paul uses in verse 7:

Trouble =

Pervert =

How does Paul describe the effects of these same false teachers in the following Scriptures?

a. Romans 16:17, 18

b. Titus 1:10, 11

6. What lessons did you learn from today's study and how will it make a difference in how you live this week?

7. Continue to work on memorizing Galatians 1:9. Can you record it below without looking?

DAY 5 – BEGIN IN PRAYER

1. Read Galatians 1.

2. Re-read Galatians 1:8-9.

3. Two times in two verses Paul calls for *anathema*: destruction for anyone who would seek to introduce, preach, or persuade others of another gospel (which Paul declared to be no gospel at all) other than the true Gospel of Jesus Christ by which they had been saved. The same Greek word is translated *bound* in Acts 23:14. What is the context in which it is used?

The truth will always outrank the credentials of the messenger. How does the story in 1Kings 13:1-25 illustrate this truth and Paul's warning to the church?

4. The enemy that wiped out the man of God in 1Kings is still alive and well today. What is his plan of attack according to 1Peter 5:8?

What clear direction for protection is given for us to follow in 2John 1:10, 11?

5. Paul repeats himself because of the serious nature of his message. To make himself absolutely clear he tells them, I have said it before and I will say it again – nothing or no one can change the message of the Gospel. He says, *"but even if we, or an angel from heaven, preach any other gospel to you than what we have preached to you, let him be accursed."* How or why is this strong judgment pronounced in the following Scriptures?

a. 1Corinthians 12:3

b. 1Corinthians 16:22

How did Paul use the word *accursed* in Romans 9:3 to show his great love for his brethren?

Follow the use of the word *cherem* (*an accursed thing, a thing devoted, dedicated or appointed to utter destruction*) in Hebrew through these passages in the Old Testament.

(If you are not familiar with this account take the time to read Joshua 6:17 – Joshua 7:26)

   a. Joshua 6:17, 18

   b. Joshua 7:10-13

   c. Joshua 7:25, 26 (The consequences of their sin)

6.   What lessons did you learn from today's study, and how will it make a difference in how you live this week?

7.   Continue to work on memorizing Galatians 1:9.

DAY 6 – BEGIN IN PRAYER

1.   Read Galatians 1. (It is very important!)

2.   Re-read Galatians 1:1-9.

3.   How would you summarize the truth taught in verses 1-9?

4.   What truth has made a difference in your walk with the Lord this week?

5.   Can you record Galatians 1:9 in the space below without looking at it? If not, continue to work on it today until you can.

DAY 1 ~ BEGIN IN PRAYER

1. Read Galatians 1.

2. Re-read Galatians 1:10-24.

3. What is the main point Paul is making in this portion of Galatians 1?

4. Why do you think it was important for the Galatian churches to understand Paul's calling? What argument would they have been using against his teaching and authority?

5. Who was Paul seeking to please in the course of his ministry and life?

Do you think it is possible to be a man pleaser and a God pleaser?

6. Your memory verse for this week is Galatians 1:10. Record it below and begin committing it to memory today.

DAY 2 ~ BEGIN IN PRAYER

1. Read Galatians 1.

2. Re-read Galatians 1:10-12.

3. After twice declaring a curse on anyone who would preach another gospel (v. 9), what statement, in the form of a question, does Paul ask regarding the motive and catalyst behind his ministry?

If Paul had been seeking to gain the approval of men, he would have only needed to continue persecuting the church because this was very popular, and it was in this action he found great support. But, the Lord had a different plan

by GRACE, be FREE

for this man's life! What does Proverbs 29:25 teach us that might have been a source of strength to Paul?

How do the following two examples illustrate the *fear of man*?

a. Genesis 12:11-20

b. Matthew 26:69-74

4.   How can the following truths keep this reccurring *fear of men* from plaguing your life?

a. Proverbs 1:7

b. Proverbs 8:13

c. Proverbs 10:27

d. Proverbs 14:26, 27

Instead of being concerned about pleasing men or finding glory from men, Paul obeyed the dramatic calling of the Lord on his life and he declares himself to be a *bondservant* of Christ. How does Exodus 21:5, 6 define the term *bondservant*?

5. In Galatians 1:11 and 12, what does Paul declare about the origin of the Gospel which he had received?

In these verses Paul clearly states the theme of his letter. His point is that his message and his ministry are of divine origin. He did not invent it, nor did he receive it from men – *it came through the revelation of Jesus Christ*. Use a Dictionary of New Testament Words to define *revelation* in verse 12.

6. What specific lesson(s) did you learn from today's study and how will it make a difference in how you live this week?

7. Continue to work on memorizing Galatians 1:10 for this week. Do not neglect this important part of the study.

DAY 3 – BEGIN IN PRAYER

1. Read Galatians 1.

2. Re-read Galatians 1:13-14.

3. It is one thing to claim inspiration and revelation, and another thing to actually prove it. Paul begins to speak first of his past, and remind the Galatian Christians of the way God had dealt with him. He describes his former standing and activities in persecuting the church as a negative proof that his message of grace had not been born out of his past pursuits. He was zealous toward the Law and vehemently persecuted all those who opposed it. Record the descriptions of his prior actions.

    a. Acts 8:1-3

    b. Acts 9:1-2

c. Acts 22:4

d. Acts 26:9-11

4. Secondly, he declares his unparalleled passion and zeal for traditional Judaism. How does Paul describe his previous attitude toward the Law?

a. Acts 22:3

b. Philippians 3:4-6

5. According to Romans 3:20-22, what was Paul's message concerning the Law and grace?

In what way does the church today face the same or a similar struggle between works and grace?

6. What specific lesson(s) did you learn from today's study and how will it make a difference in how you live this week?

7. Continue to work on memorizing Galatians 1:10 for this week.

DAY 4 – BEGIN IN PRAYER

1. Read Galatians 1.

2. Re-read Galatians 1:15-17.

3. Paul changes the subject from his past character and conduct, and now begins

to speak of his conversion. What does verse 15 teach us about the timing and method involved in Paul's conversion?

There was definitely no human explanation for the 180-degree transformation in every aspect of Paul's life. He was without control and without restraint and fully committed to the destruction of the church. Then, he came face-to-face with Jesus Christ on the road to Damascus (Acts 9:5). According to verse 15, when did this calling in Paul's life actually occur?

What more do you learn about the calling and election of God's children?

    a. Deuteronomy 7:7, 8

    b. 1Samuel 12:22

    c. Jeremiah 1:5

    d. Romans 8:29, 30

    e. Ephesians 1:3-6

4. The Lord had set Paul apart for salvation and apostleship even before he was born. Paul says that this calling from God was a calling by *grace*. Use a Dictionary of New Testament Words to define the word grace in verse 15.

What was Paul's clearly defined calling and who was he to deliver his message to (v. 16a)?

What is the calling and message of the church today?

a. Mark 16:15, 16

b. Romans 10:14, 15

c. 1Peter 2:9

5. At the end of verse 16 Paul writes that he did not immediately seek counsel or direction from men. In fact, he headed for the desert. His first move was to spend time alone with God. It was very important that the Lord establish Paul's independence as an apostle. He was not taught by the other apostles but would be fully equal to them. Paul may have spent the major part of three years alone with the Lord in the desert of Arabia. The other disciples had received three years of teaching from the Lord Jesus, and now it was Paul's turn. What other Biblical leaders spent time in the desert in preparation for ministry?

6. What specific lesson(s) did you learn from today's study and how will it make a difference in how you live this week?

7. Continue to work on memorizing Galatians 1:10 for this week.

DAY 5 – BEGIN IN PRAYER

1. Read Galatians 1.

2. Re-read Galatians 1:18-24.

3. Let's follow the footsteps of Paul during these early years of his calling. Locate the Arabian Desert, the city of Damascus, and the regions of Syria and Cilicia on a Bible map. Compare these areas to a modern day map. What country

or countries was Paul traveling through?

Describe Paul's first ministry opportunities in Damascus as recorded in Acts 9:20-25.

What was the response and outcome?

4. After escaping from Damascus, Paul headed to Jerusalem. Imagine what it might have been like for him to return to a place where he had severely persecuted the church. He had imprisoned or killed husbands, wives, children or parents of many of these surviving believers. What was Paul's welcome like in Jerusalem according to Acts 9:26-29?

    As a result of this death threat, Paul was ushered to the coast city of Caesarea, and then to his hometown of Tarsus. (Acts 9:30) Paul's point is: he had no close ties with the church in Jerusalem or the churches of Judea and he was called and commissioned by the Lord Jesus Christ Himself to be an apostle. What proof do we find in the following verses to demonstrate that the Apostles accepted Paul's calling as genuine?

    a. Acts 15:22-27

    b. 2Peter 3:15, 16

5. Paul's conclusion is this – it was obvious from his past, his conversion and his ministry, that God alone had made him who they saw and knew. In time they came to believe his conversion to be true. What was the result of that belief according to Galatians 1:24?

    According to the following Scriptures, what actions of the early church caused the Lord to be glorified?

    a. Acts 21:19-20a

b. 2Corinthians 9:10-15

c. 2Thessalonians 1:11, 12

What very bright exhortation is given to you, as a Christian in a very dark world, in Matthew 5:14-16?

Personal: How brightly are you shining? How much glory is your Heavenly Father receiving as others observe your life? What changes need to be made?

6. What specific lesson(s) did you learn from today's study and how will it make a difference in how you live this week?

7. Continue to work on memorizing Galatians 1:10 for this week.

DAY 6 – BEGIN IN PRAYER

1. Read Galatians 1. (It is very important!)

2. Re-read Galatians 1:10-24.

3. How would you summarize the truth taught in verses 10-24?

4. What truth has made a difference in your walk with the Lord this week?

5. Can you record Galatians 1:10 in the space below without looking at it? If not, continue to work on it today until you can.

DAY 1 – BEGIN IN PRAYER

1. Read Galatians 2.

2. Re-read Galatians 2:1-10.

3. What prompted Paul's trip to Jerusalem (v. 2)?

4. In this chapter Paul continues his defense of the Gospel, and of his God-given authority to preach it to the Gentiles, by relating the account of a trip to Jerusalem. What main point is made clear in these verses regarding his calling and relationship to the human authorities in the Jerusalem church?

5. Who were these *pillars* of authority?

6. Your memory verse for this week is Galatians 2:5. Record it below and begin committing it to memory today.

DAY 2 – BEGIN IN PRAYER
(Don't forget Who your Teacher is!)

1. Read Galatians 2.

2. Re-read Galatians 2:1.

3. Last week Paul spoke of his life prior to salvation, his salvation, and his three-year seminary study in the desert where he received the Gospel from the Lord Himself. Now he takes a leap ahead and tells us about a time the Lord sent him up to Jerusalem. Who did he take with him?

4. What do you learn about Barnabas from the following Scriptures?

by **GRACE,**
be **Free**

a. Acts 4:36, 37

b. Acts 9:26, 27

c. Acts 11:22-26

d. Acts 13:1-7

e. Acts 15:36-39

What strong spiritual characteristics are evident in Titus' life?

a. Titus 1:4

b. 2Corinthians 7:6, 7

c. 2Corinthians 8:16, 17

d. 2Corinthians 8:23

5. This God-led journey that took Paul up to Jerusalem is covered in great detail in Acts 15:1-31. Record a few summary details of this Jerusalem council meeting.

6. What specific lesson(s) did you learn from today's study and how will it make a difference in how you live this week?

7. Continue to work on memorizing Galatians 2:5 for this week. Do not neglect this important part of the study.

DAY 3 – BEGIN IN PRAYER

1. Read Galatians 2.

2. Re-read Galatians 2:2-5.

3. After Paul's first missionary journey, he and Barnabas returned to Antioch and reported to the church how the Lord had opened the doors of faith unto the Gentiles (Acts 14:27). This news did not sit well with the Jewish legalists of Jerusalem, so they came to Antioch and began teaching that before a Gentile became a Christian he must first become a Jew. This would mean mandatory circumcision and submission to the whole Jewish Law. It was this clash that took Paul, Barnabas and Titus to Jerusalem by the leading of the Holy Spirit. With whom did they have their first meeting?

    Why do you think Paul went to meet privately with the church leaders rather than seeking to speak before the entire church first?

    What do you think Paul meant by the phrase *lest by any means I might run, or had run, in vain*?

    What do you learn from the following Scriptures that help you to understand Paul's comment in Galatians 2:2?

    a. Galatians 4:8-11

b. Philippians 2:14-16

c. 1 Thessalonians 3:5

4. Paul uses the acceptance of Titus as proof that the leaders of the Jerusalem church applied none of the pressure or made none of the demands on him that the Judaizers were advocating. What was Titus not compelled to do?

According to Acts 15:1, 5, what was the teaching of the *false brethren* who brought these charges against Paul?

For the record, how was this false doctrine introduced into the church (Galatians 2:4)?

What warning is given in these verses to the church regarding these false teachers?

a. Acts 20:29-30

b. 2 Corinthians 11:13-15

c. 1 John 4:1-3

d. 2 Peter 2:1, 2

5. Paul boldly stood firm against these *false brethren* and their false doctrine of mixing the law with grace. It cannot be done. They are mutually exclusive. He declares that he *did not yield in submission* (to the legalistic bondage of the

Judaizers) *even for an hour.* In regards to method of ministry, Paul became *all things to all men, that he might by all means save some* (1 Corinthians 9:22). But in matters of doctrine relating to the heart of the Gospel, he would not be moved one inch from the truth. Should the believer ever allow errors of the basic doctrine of salvation to stand unchallenged?

What guidance is given to us when bold defense of the Gospel is necessary?

a. Ephesians 4:11-16

b. Colossians 4:5, 6

6.   What specific lesson(s) did you learn from today's study and how will it make a difference in how you live this week?

7.   Continue to work on memorizing Galatians 2:5 for this week.

DAY 4 ~ BEGIN IN PRAYER

1.   Read Galatians 2.

2.   Re-read Galatians 2:6-8.

3.   Paul makes it clear that he did not need the approval of these leaders in Jerusalem or any other man. He knew, and was absolutely certain, that his calling and commission was from the Lord Himself. In verse 6, he twice refers to the apostles as *those who seemed to be something.* He was not slighting the godly ministry of these men but rather addressing the accusations of the Judaizers who accused him of being a self-appointed and inferior apostle. Paul didn't need man's approval, he had God's word and His approval. How does 1 Thessalonians 2:3-5 support this truth?

According to 1 Corinthians 2:3-5, how does Paul describe his demeanor among the people and what was it that caused his preaching to be so effective?

4. In verse 6, Paul tells us that God *shows personal favoritism to no man*. The other apostles and leaders of the church had no greater access to the Lord, no greater power than other faithful servants and no greater authority to preach the Gospel. How are we sometimes tempted to set some people above others or above ourselves, showing favoritism toward them? Give some examples.

What does the Word tell us about *partiality and personal favoritism* and how will these truths change the way you make choices and handle decisions from now on?

a. 2Chronicles 19:5-7

b. Job 34:19

c. Proverbs 24:23

d. Acts 10:34, 35

e. 1Peter 1:17-19

5. Paul continues, *"on the contrary, they saw clearly that the Lord had commissioned me to take the Gospel to the Gentiles (uncircumcised)."* It is clear that Paul is not speaking of two different messages only two different spheres of ministry. God has a specific calling and area of ministry for each member of the Body of Christ. Paul was to go to the Gentiles but this did not restrict him from preaching the Gospel to the Jews when he had the opportunity. In fact, in most cities he entered he went first to the synagogues with the Good News. Likewise, Peter preached mainly to the Jews, but was free to share with whoever would hear and listen. So it is in the Body of Christ today. Each of

us has a part – are you doing yours? What is it?

What do we learn about the ministry of the Body of Christ in 1Corinthians 12:12-26?

The following references speak of some of the various ministries the Lord may call us to use so that the Body of Christ will function perfectly and shine brightly to the lost in this world. List them and as you do – ask the Lord to reveal His calling upon your life!

a. Romans 12:6-8

b. 1Corinthians 12:7-11

c. 1Corinthians 12:27, 28

d. 2Corinthians 5:20

e. Mark 16:15

6. What specific lesson(s) did you learn from today's study and how will it make a difference in how you live this week?

7. Continue to work on memorizing Galatians 2:5 for this week.

DAY 5 – BEGIN IN PRAYER

1. Read Galatians 2.

2. Re-read Galatians 2:9-10.

3. It is clear that Paul was accepted and received by the leadership in Jerusalem. Not only was their message the same, their mission was the same. They would be taking the Gospel of grace to the entire world – Jew and Gentile. They were in personal harmony and this must have infuriated the Judaizers who had come to Jerusalem for support for their false teaching and found none. What was the final decision of the Jerusalem council according Acts 15:13-29?

4. The *right hand of fellowship* describes the method in the Near East of committing a solemn vow of friendship and it was a mark of fellowship or partnership. How important it is that the church is in unity within and how tragic that division is probably one of the most successful tools used by the enemy to destroy our effectiveness as witnesses to the world. What do we learn about the importance of unity in the Body of Christ?

    a. Psalm 133:1

    b. John 13:34, 35

    c. Philippians 2:2-5

    d. 1 Thessalonians 3:12

    e. 1 Peter 3:8, 9

5. What was the only request that was made of Paul and Barnabas (v. 10)?

    This request was not doctrinal, but practical. It was a reminder of the needs of the brethren in Jerusalem who were very poor because of the onslaught of persecution of the church. What was Paul's response to this request?

What clear direction is given to us regarding the physical needs of those who are struggling?

a. 1 Timothy 6:17-19

b. 1 John 3:16-18

c. James 2:15-17

Personal: Is there a way that you could be helping someone who is in need? It doesn't have to be an extravagant gift – maybe some of your time, a cup of coffee or a bit of help not asked for! You will be as blessed in the giving as they are in the receiving!

6. What specific lesson(s) did you learn from today's study and how will it make a difference in how you live this week?

7. Continue to work on memorizing Galatians 2:5 for this week.

DAY 6 – BEGIN IN PRAYER

1. Read Galatians 2. (It is very important!)

2. Re-read Galatians 2:1-10.

3. How would you summarize the truth taught in verses 1-10?

4. What truth has made a difference in your walk with the Lord this week?

5.   Can you record Galatians 2:5 in the space below without looking at it? If not, continue to work on it today until you can.

DAY 1 ~ BEGIN IN PRAYER

1. Read Galatians 2.

2. Re-read Galatians 2:11-21.

3. What incident does Paul describe in this portion of chapter 2 that strengthens his credibility as a true apostle of the Lord Jesus Christ?

4. What strong word does Paul use to describe Peter's actions in verse 13?

5. What is your definition of *hypocrisy* and how have you seen it show itself in your life and walk with Jesus?

6. Your memory verse for this week is Galatians 2:20. Record it below and begin committing it to memory today.

DAY 2 ~ BEGIN IN PRAYER

1. Read Galatians 2:11-21.

2. Re-read Galatians 2:11-13.

3. Sometime after the council meeting in Jerusalem, which is recorded in Acts 15, Peter traveled from Jerusalem to Antioch. What took place?

What was the result of Peter's actions in the lives of those who looked up to him?

What was Paul's response?

by **GRACE,** be **free**

What do you think would have been the affect of Peter's choice on the church at Antioch if Paul had not confronted him?

4. Paul declares, *"I withstood him to his face, because he was to be blamed."* Peter knew very well that the freedom to enjoy fellowship with the Gentile believers was God ordained, yet he withdrew because of the opinion of others. What are we told in the following verses that will help us when we face a choice like Peter did?

a. Proverbs 29:25, 26

b. Matthew 10:28-33

c. John 12:42, 43

How does the account of a wrong choice in Abraham's life recorded in Genesis 12:11-20 illustrate the same lesson we are learning today?

Personal: Have you been faced with a similar choice in your walk lately? How did you respond? What will you say or do differently next time? Ask the Lord to empower you with His Holy Spirit so that you are able to boldly stand up for truth.

5. Use a Dictionary of Bible Words to define the words *hypocrite* and *hypocrisy* as used in verse 13.

What does the Bible teach us about hypocrisy in the following references?

a. Luke 12:1-3

    b. Romans 12:9

    c. James 3:17

    d. 1 Peter 2:1-3

Peter's hypocrisy affected far more than his own walk with the Lord. *When certain men came from James*, Peter withdrew himself from fellowship with the Gentiles *because he feared those who were of the circumcision*. In doing so, many others followed his example, including Barnabas. This account of Peter's failure shows us that anyone is capable of falling, and of causing others to stumble. Faithfulness requires more than right believing; it must produce right behavior or it is hypocrisy. In your life, who is watching your behavior and following your example?

Are they seeing a gospel of rules or the gospel of grace?

6.   What specific lesson(s) did you learn from today's study and how will it make a difference in how you live this week?

7.   Continue to work on memorizing Galatians 2:20 for this week. Be careful not to neglect this important part of the study.

DAY 3 – BEGIN IN PRAYER

1.   Read Galatians 2:11-21.

2.   Re-read Galatians 2:14-16.

3. How did Paul choose to deal with the inconsistency and sin observed in Peter's life?

Why do you think this public rebuke was necessary?

What exhortation did Paul later write to Pastor Timothy in 1 Timothy 5:19-21 that better explains Paul's actions here in Antioch?

4. Paul did not tolerate anything that threatened the integrity of the Gospel. He straightforwardly asked Peter this question, *"if you, being a Jew, live in the manner of Gentiles and not as the Jews, why do you compel Gentiles to live as Jews?"* There was definitely a serious problem with Peter's actions. In society today, and sadly in the church as well, there is a popular trend that calls for unity regardless of belief. This is the exact opposite of the way Paul led the early church. What direction are we given in Ephesians 4:15, 16 that will guide us in dealing with conflict in our churches today?

The truth that Paul was protecting is the heart of the Gospel. Our salvation is by grace through faith in the competed work of Jesus Christ at Calvary (Ephesians 2:8, 9). The Law could not bring salvation. Paul declared that the Jews were God's chosen people by birth and yet having lived under the Law these believers had come to realize their need to accept Jesus Christ as their Lord and Savior. What more can we learn about the Law?

a. Romans 8:2, 3

b. Romans 9:30-32

c. Romans 10:4

d. Galatians 3:24-26

5. Paul gives us the most clear and forceful statement regarding the doctrine of justification found in the New Testament. Use a Dictionary of New Testament Words to define *justified* from verse 16.

Use the following Scriptures to help you learn the full meaning of the doctrine of justification.

a. Romans 5:1, 2

b. Romans 5:18

c. Romans 8:33, 34

d. Romans 4:1-8

Personal: Knowing these things to be absolute truth – how will truly trusting God at His Word bring new freedom to your life? What accusations of the enemy are proven to be no longer valid? Praise the Lord for His finished work of making you, as His child, justified. It is easy to remember it this way, justified means, "Just as if I had NEVER sinned."

6. What specific lesson(s) did you learn from today's study and how will it make a difference in how you live this week?

7. Continue to work on memorizing Galatians 2:20 for this week. Can you record it below without looking?

DAY 4 – BEGIN IN PRAYER

1. Read Galatians 2:11-21.

2. Re-read Galatians 2:17-19.

3. Paul continues, "Peter, if as your actions say, eating with Gentiles is a sin, wouldn't Christ Himself be implicated because it was He who instructed you to do so?" Read and review Acts 10. Record a few important details.

    Is there anything in your life that you are calling *unclean* that the Lord does not?

4. Peter's actions of separating himself from fellowship with the Gentiles were rebuilding a wall that the Lord had instructed the early church to destroy or tear down. To do this was truly a transgression against God's clear command. In other words, if anyone, even Paul or Peter, tries to rebuild a system of legalism after he has once destroyed it by believing and preaching the gospel of God's grace, he proves himself, not Christ, to be a transgressor. Compare Galatians 2:19 with Romans 7:1-6. What clear point is made in each of the following verses in Romans 7?

    Verse 1

    Verse 2

    Verse 3

    Verse 4

    Verse 5

    Verse 6

5. Paul declares the law is no longer a factor in his life. He had tried to live by it and all it taught him was that he was sinful and weak and that he needed a Savior. He therefore, died to the law *that he might live to God*. How do the following Scriptures characterize the life that is *lived to God*?

a. Psalm 104:33, 34

b. Colossians 3:1-4

c. 1 Peter 1:3-9

d. 1 John 2:15-17

6. What specific lesson(s) did you learn from today's study and how will it make a difference in how you live this week?

7. Continue to work on memorizing Galatians 2:20 for this week. Can you record it below without looking?

DAY 5 – BEGIN IN PRAYER

1. Read Galatians 2:11-21

2. Re-read Galatians 2:20-21.

3. Paul testifies to an awesome truth in the believer's life, our old life was crucified along with Christ on the cross at Calvary. We were slaves to sin, we had no other option. However, with Christ's death and resurrection we became alive to righteousness in Jesus Christ. We now have a choice whether to sin or not to sin. What do we learn about this new life in Christ from Romans 6:1-18? Record a few details that speak to your heart today.

Personal: Have you been living as a slave to sin, or as a slave to righteousness?

4. Paul declares, *I have been crucified with Christ; it is not longer I who live, but Christ lives in me.* What does it mean to you personally to be *crucified with Christ?*

What do the following Scriptures teach us about the life of this new man in which Christ lives and reigns?

a. Colossians 3:9, 10

b. Colossians 3:12-14

c. Romans 13:12-14

d. Ephesians 4:20-24

e. 1 Peter 1:13-16

5. We, like Paul, *are to live by faith in the Son of God.* We do not have faith for faith's sake or faith in fate, but we have faith in the finished work of Jesus Christ on the cross at Calvary, which paid the penalty for our every sin. He loves you! It is a statement of fact. He gave Himself to pay the debt for your sin! Legalism's most destructive effect is that it makes the cross of no effect. Paul tells us, if we, like Peter, set aside the grace of God for works of righteousness, then Christ's death would be for nothing. What does Paul write about the vital importance of the cross?

a. 1 Corinthians 1:18

b. 1 Corinthians 1:23, 24

c. 1 Corinthians 2:1-5

6. What specific lesson(s) did you learn from today's study and how will it make a difference in how you live this week?

7. Continue to work on memorizing Galatians 2:20 for this week. Can you record it below without looking?

DAY 6 – BEGIN IN PRAYER

1. Read Galatians 2.

2. Re-read Galatians 2:11-21.

3. How would you summarize the truth taught in verses 11-21?

4. What truth has made a difference in your walk with the Lord this week?

5. Can you record Galatians 2:20 in the space below without looking at it? If not, continue to work on it today until you can.

40

DAY 1 – BEGIN IN PRAYER

1. Read Galatians 3.

2. Re-read Galatians 3:1-14.

3. Paul changes the focus of his letter at this point. He first spoke about his personal experience with God's grace, now he delivers a very clear doctrinal instruction about grace. What strong adjective does he use to describe those in Galatia who were turning from grace back to the Law? (vs. 1-3)

4. In these fourteen verses Paul gives us a series of contrasts to help prove his point. List as many as you can.

5. What is the main point(s) that Paul is trying to establish in this passage of Scripture?

6. Your memory verse for this week is Galatians 3:3. Record it below and begin committing it to memory today.

DAY 2 – BEGIN IN PRAYER

1. Read Galatians 3:1-14.

2. Re-read Galatians 3:1-3.

3. The history of the church is filled with believers falling prey to legalism in their relationship with God. In chapters 1 and 2 Paul spoke of his personal experience with grace, in his life and in his ministry. Now he addresses the personal conversion of the believers in Galatia. He begins by asking them a

series of pointed questions. What is the first one found in verse 1?

Use a Dictionary of New Testament Words to define the following words in verse 1.

a. Foolish

b. Bewitched

How are those who would seek to bewitch you with teaching contrary to the Scriptures described in the following verses?

a. 2Corinthians 11:3, 4

b. 2Corinthians 11:12-15

c. 2Peter 2:18, 19

4.   Paul had come to the region of Galatia boldly declaring Jesus Christ – crucified, buried and raised from the dead. It is through His finished work of salvation by grace through faith that we can obtain salvation. Nothing need be, **nor can be,** added to this finished work!   Yet many in Galatia were being bewitched. Paul calls them foolish. This word does not mean that they were mentally deficient but they were being lazy and careless with the truth of the Gospel. Paul takes them back to the beginning of their faith. What question does he ask in verse 2?

How about you, were you saved by works or by the hearing of faith?

Are you ever tempted to rely on the works of the flesh to bring you closer to the Lord? If yes, how or why?

How do the following examples stand as a reminder that will help keep you from returning to that from which you have been set free?

a. Acts 10:34-45

b. Acts 16:28-34

What clear declaration of truth is given to you in Titus 3:4-7 and how will knowing this truth change the way you think and act today?

5.   Paul continues with the probing questions in verse 3. What two questions does He ask them (and us)?

If salvation comes only by God's grace, what makes us think something more is now required of us in order to grow and become mature (perfect in Christ)? To the best of your knowledge, describe the following systems of works righteousness (what might they say that you should add to grace).

a. Formalism

b. Legalism

c. Spiritualism

How does Luke 5:1-11 speak about the fruitfulness of a work in the Spirit compared with the work of the flesh?

6. What specific lesson(s) did you learn from today's study and how will it make a difference in how you live this week?

7. Continue to work on memorizing Galatians 3:3 for this week. Be careful not to neglect this important part of the study.

DAY 3 – BEGIN IN PRAYER

1. Read Galatians 3:1-14.

2. Re-read Galatians 3:4-5.

3. Choosing to follow the Lord Jesus Christ had certainly brought extreme criticism, opposition and rejection to the lives of these believers. Paul poses a fifth question to these wayward people. What is it? (v.4)

    According to Paul, they had believed whole-heartedly and were committed enough to suffer many things because of their faith, but something had changed – would it all be in vain – would it all be for nothing? What encouragement and warning is written in Hebrews 10:32-39 regarding staying the course and making it to the end?

4. Good works do not increase our standing before God, nor elevate us to a higher spiritual status. As a believer, you are a child of God and fellow heir with Jesus Christ, who is the Heir to all things. You can't reach a higher level, or gain greater acceptance than this! What do the following Scriptures teach you about your position in Jesus Christ?

a. Romans 8:16, 17

b. Galatians 4:4-7

Paul softens his statement by adding, *if indeed it was in vain?* He sincerely prayed that they would correct their current direction and return to grace. Have you ever had to strongly defend the truth of the Gospel to anyone you loved who was going astray?

If, in the future you do, will you be willing to risk the relationship for the restoration?

What guidelines are we given to follow from the Word of God?

a. Galatians 6:1, 2

b. Ephesians 4:15

c. Jude 1:21-23

d. James 5:19, 20

5. In Galatians 3:5 the pronoun *He* is referring to God, the Father. Paul's last question to his readers is, when God supplies the Spirit to you and works miracles among you, is He doing this out of love, by the Spirit, or on the merit system of good works? For the record, what is your answer?

Personal: Yes or no? If you pray more today, read more today, witness more today or hold your temper better today, will the Lord bless you more, love you more and answer your prayers quicker? Why or why not?

For the sake of balance, what does praying more, reading more, witnessing more and being more obedient to the Word of the Lord prove about your salvation through grace by faith in Jesus Christ?

What does James 2:14, 17 and 24 say about a faith that produces no fruit?

These good works in our lives are verifying, not producing, salvation in our hearts!

6.   What specific lesson(s) did you learn from today's study and how will it make a difference in how you live this week?

7.   Continue to work on memorizing Galatians 3:3 for this week. Can you record it below without looking?

DAY 4 – BEGIN IN PRAYER

1.   Read Galatians 3:1-14.

2.   Re-read Galatians 3:6-9.

3.   From the subjective look of personal experience Paul now turns to the more objective study of grace according to the Word of God. Paul had asked six questions in verses 1-5 and here he follows them with six quotes and examples from the Old Testament. By these he proves to his readers that salvation is given wholly by the grace of God. He begins with the faith of Father Abraham. Let's follow his walk of faith through Genesis. Record what you learn.

a. Genesis 12:1-4

b. Genesis 13:14-17

c. Genesis 15:2-6

d. Genesis 17:1-11

The Judaizers were teaching that the Gentiles needed to believe in Jesus Christ and be circumcised and follow the Law of Moses in order to truly be saved. This is not what God commanded or intended. God had given circumcision to the people to identify them and protect them from the pagan people they were exposed to. It was an external, physical act that had no redeeming power in itself. According to the above Scriptures, *did Abraham believe God and it was accounted to him for righteousness* before or after God gave the Covenant of circumcision to Abraham?

4.   Paul continues to prove his point by concluding that *only those who are of faith are sons of Abraham*. Read Romans 4:1-16 and record a few details about God's grace and true faith.

What strong words did John the Baptist have for the religious leaders coming to him to be baptized without repentance? (Luke 3:7-9)

5.   Paul points to this promise of God to Abraham in Genesis 12:3, *in you all the nations shall be blessed* and he declares that it is the best of news to the Galatian church and to us today! From the very beginning of Abraham's relationship with God, the blessing of salvation was promised to all the nations of the world. If you have placed your faith in the finished work of Jesus Christ at Calvary, then you are included with those spoken of in verse 9. You are truly blessed with believing Abraham. What are those blessings?

a. Ephesians 1:3-7

b. Ephesians 2:4-7

c. Revelation 5:9, 10

With the fresh knowledge of just a few of the blessings the Lord has bestowed upon your life, write a prayer of praise for His goodness and blessing to you!

6. What specific lesson(s) did you learn from today's study and how will it make a difference in how you live this week?

7. Continue to work on memorizing Galatians 3:3 for this week. How are you doing on it?

DAY 5 – BEGIN IN PRAYER

1. Read Galatians 3:1-14.

2. Re-read Galatians 3:10-14.

3. In verse 10, Paul quotes Deuteronomy 27:26, making the point that the Law demands perfect obedience, and this means obedience in **all things**. The Law was a curse because it clearly made the point that man was sinful and deserving of judgment. According to the judgment of God in regards to sin (law-breaking), one offense or transgression brings the full wrath of the Law upon the sinner. So just as circumcision didn't save, neither did the Law. Rather it illustrated the need for a Savior. What do the following Scriptures teach us about the purpose of the Law?

a. Galatians 3:24-26

b. Hebrews 10:1-10

c. Acts 13:38, 39

4. The next point in Paul's argument is that since no one is justified by the law in the sight of God, it is evident that *the just shall live by faith*. Who was the first to speak these words of truth and what was the circumstance according to Habakkuk 2:4?

What exhortation and encouragement are found in the following references in which this same truth is declared?

a. Romans 1:16, 17

b. Hebrews 10:36-39

5. The good news of the finished work of Jesus Christ at Calvary is that *Christ has redeemed us from the curse of the law, having become a curse for us!* The word *redeemed* is commonly used of buying a slave's freedom. These last two verses (13-14) beautifully summarize all that Paul has been teaching us! The price has been paid for our **every** sin! The sinless Son of God was the only One who was able to pay the penalty demanded by the Law and He did it for you! He did it that *we might receive the promise of the Spirit through faith!* Refresh your memory regarding the awesome blessings you have been given in Jesus Christ by reading and meditating on the following Scriptures.

a. 1Corinthians 1:8,9

b. 2Corinthians 5:21

c. 1 Peter 2:24-25

Personal: Are you living by faith or still trying to fulfill the Law? Will you rest in His grace through faith in Jesus Christ and allow Him to transform you from the inside out, making you more and more like Jesus everyday?

6.   What specific lesson(s) did you learn from today's study and how will it make a difference in how you live this week?

7.   Continue to work on memorizing Galatians 3:3 for this week.

DAY 6 – BEGIN IN PRAYER

1.   Read Galatians 3.

2.   Re-read Galatians 3:1-14.

3.   How would you summarize the truth taught in verses 1-14?

4.   What truth has made a difference in your walk with the Lord this week?

5.   Can you record Galatians 3:3 in the space below without looking at it? If not, continue to work on it today until you can.

DAY 1 – BEGIN IN PRAYER

1.   Read Galatians 3.

2.   Re-read Galatians 3:15-29.

3.   According to this portion of Galatians 3, what is the purpose of the Law?

4.   How are we made sons and daughters of God?

5.   What is the main point(s) that Paul is trying to establish in this passage of Scripture?

6.   Your memory verse for this week is Galatians 3:24. Record it below and begin committing it to memory today.

DAY 2 – BEGIN IN PRAYER

1.   Read Galatians 3:15-29. (Don't skip this important part!)

2.   Re-read Galatians 3:15-18.

3.   In Galatians 3:1-14 Paul had given proof from the Old Testament Scriptures that Abraham was justified by faith and not by the Law. By this he concludes that every other believer, whether Jew or Gentile, is likewise saved **only** by faith in the finished work of Jesus Christ. He begins his further proofs by speaking of a simple pact, agreement, or **covenant** between two men. If two individuals, or parties, sign a legal contract, who can make changes to it?

Re-read Genesis 12:1-3 and Genesis 15:1-6. Was this a two-party agreement or did all the responsibility for the success of the covenant fall on one party?

— by GRACE,
be Free

Whose responsibility was it to uphold the covenant between Abraham and God?

4. God ratified the covenant between He and Abraham by participating in a ceremony common to the ancient Near East. Describe the ceremony according to Genesis 15:7-18.

Who walked in the midst of the slain animals?

Ordinarily, both parties to a covenant would walk between the slain animals, thus agreeing to a blood oath that could not be altered or set aside. What was Abraham doing when the LORD, symbolically walked in the midst of the animals?

This covenant was based solely on the faithfulness of God and His promises toward Abraham. In the same manner, there is a New Covenant in place today that also depends solely upon the Lord's finished sacrifice. What do we learn about this New Covenant from the following Scripture references?

a. Matthew 26:28

b. Luke 22:20

c. 1 Corinthians 11:25

d. Hebrews 9:15

5. Since all the responsibility of the covenant between God and Abraham fell on God, all Abraham had to do was to accept the promises made to him through

the covenant. We read in Galatians 3:16 that it was to Abraham and his Seed, speaking of Christ, that this promise was made. Therefore, even the giving of the Law could not annul the promise. As believers in Jesus Christ, we have inherited the blessings of the New Covenant. Are you aware of the promises God has made to you through Jesus Christ? He is ever faithful; He does not change; His Word abides forever! Therefore you, like Abraham, can rest in His faithfulness! List as many of the promises that God has given to the church as you can.

Add these to your list, if you haven't already thought of them.

a. Matthew 6:32-33

b. John 15:9-17

c. Romans 8:28, 29

d. Hebrews 13:5, 6

e. 1 John 5:11-15

6. What specific lesson(s) did you learn from today's study and how will it make a difference in how you live this week?

7. Continue to work on memorizing Galatians 3:24 for this week. Be careful not to neglect this important part of the study.

DAY 3 – BEGIN IN PRAYER

1. Read Galatians 3:15-29.

2. Re-read Galatians 3:19-20.

3. Paul's point to his readers is that God made this covenant of promise with Abraham *through Christ*. No one except God the Father and God the Son could alter the promise. Moses could not alter it and neither could the Judaizers who wanted to return from grace to the keeping of the Law. Perhaps, anticipating the next argument of the Judaizers, Paul answers what may have been their next question, "Why then was the Law given?" According to verse 19, what was Paul's answer?

   Use a Bible Dictionary to define the word translated *transgressions* in verse 19.

   The law was not given as a vehicle to save, but to point out our transgressions. How does Paul describe the effects of the law in his life in Romans 7:7-9?

4. According to verse 19, was the law given as a permanent or a temporary measure?

   What good news do we find in Romans regarding the fulfillment of the demands of the law?

   a. Romans 7:4-7

   b. Romans 8:1-4

What blessing is added by these words of our Lord Jesus Christ in Matthew 5:17, 18?

How does the writer of Hebrews describe the fulfillment of the law through the finished work of Jesus Christ in Hebrews 10:1-12?

5. The next point Paul makes is that the covenant of the law was inferior to the covenant of grace due to the fact that when God gave the law to the children of Israel He did so through a mediator (the angels to Moses – Acts 7:53). The covenant of grace was a result of God Himself making promises directly to Abraham, cutting out the mediator. The attempt of the Judaizers to exalt the law of Moses over God's work of grace was foolish and wrong. With so much talk of the law, let's rejoice in the truth of the following Scriptures regarding the grace we have received through Jesus Christ.

a. Ephesians 1:3-7

b. Ephesians 2:8-10

c. Romans 3:24, 25

d. Titus 3:5-7

6. What specific lesson(s) did you learn from today's study and how will it make a difference in how you live this week?

7. Continue to work on memorizing Galatians 3:24 for this week. Can you record it without looking?

DAY 4 – BEGIN IN PRAYER

1. Read Galatians 3:15-29.

2. Re-read Galatians 3:21-25.

3. The next question Paul addresses is the obvious objection of the Judaizers, *Is the law then against the promises of God?* His definitive answer is **certainly not!** The law and the promise do not contradict one another, but rather they cooperate with one another. From each of the following verses describe the purpose of the law (what it could do and what it could not do).

    a. Galatians 3:21

    b. Galatians 3:22

    c. Galatians 3:23

    d. Galatians 3:24

    e. Galatians 3:25

4. If life and righteousness could have come by the law then there would have been no reason for Christ to come to die for our sins. God gave the law so that it would become painfully obvious that man was desperately sinful and in need of a Savior. How is this truth clearly defined in the following portion of Scripture in Romans? (Do not completely write out these verses – just summarize what they are saying to you.)

a. Romans 3:9-18

b. Romans 3:19-23

5.   Before faith came, we were *confined* under sin. In Greek the word translated *confined* in verse 22 means *to shut in, or enclose on all sides, to close in completely with no way of escape.* According to Scripture, before we found grace through Jesus Christ we were prisoners of sin. The purpose of the law is to reveal and convict men of sin. It isn't until a person comes to the knowledge that he is sinful and that as a result of his sin he is condemned to death and judgment that he will truly be free to repent and call on Jesus Christ Who died for his sin. What wonderful promise is given the moment we call?

a. Romans 6:22, 23

b. Romans 10:9, 10

c. Romans 10:13

Before grace came, we were kept under guard by the law; it was our guardian and our tutor. It was not our source of life. Once we came to trust Jesus Christ as our Lord and Savior we were no longer confined by the law. We were set free by grace. The believer in Jesus Christ has been *justified by faith.* The word *justified* means *to render righteous, to declare or pronounce one to be just.*
It might help you to remember it if you think of it this way, to be justified means "just as if I had never sinned." Meditate on Romans 5:1-5 and make it a prayer of praise from your heart today.

6.   What specific lesson(s) did you learn from today's study and how will it make a difference in how you live this week?

7. Continue to work on memorizing Galatians 3:24 for this week.

DAY 5 – BEGIN IN PRAYER

1. Read Galatians 3:15-29.

2. Re-read Galatians 3:26-29.

3. Our faith in Christ Jesus brings us into an intimate family relationship with the Heavenly Father. Through faith we have access and a relationship that is not possible for anyone but the true believer in Jesus Christ. It is popular to consider that God is the Father of all humans, but this is Scripturally untrue. What do the following references teach us about our family status?

    a. John 1:12, 13

    b. Romans 8:14-17

    c. Ephesians 1:4-6

    d. 1John 3:1, 2

    There is no such loving relationship for those who reject Jesus Christ as their Lord and Savior. See Romans 5:10, Ephesians 2:3, John 8:44.

4. Paul is not speaking of physical water baptism in verse 27, but rather the spiritual identification and immersion into the life of Christ. We are to put on Christ. What do the following verses teach us about this process of *putting on Christ?*

    a. Romans 13:11-14

    b. Ephesians 4:21-24

    c. Colossians 3:9-10

    What is our responsibility in this process?

    Personal: What practical action are you taking daily to put off the old nature and put on Christ?

5. With this new relationship comes a new family. In the Body of Christ we are all equal, all accepted, all one. We all came with the same credentials, filthy rags, and therefore, we are to be living and serving Jesus as one. Since we belong to Jesus we have been grafted into Abraham's family of faith according to the promise. According to Ephesians 4:25-32, how then ought we to live?

6. What specific lesson(s) did you learn from today's study and how will it make a difference in how you live this week?

7. Continue to work on memorizing Galatians 3:24 for this week.

DAY 6 – BEGIN IN PRAYER

1. Read Galatians 3.

2. Re-read Galatians 3:15-29.

3.   How would you summarize the truth taught in verses 15-29?

4.   What truth has made a difference in your walk with the Lord this week?

5.   Can you record Galatians 3:24 in the space below without looking at it? If not, continue to work on it today until you can.

> "THE LAW CANNOT CHANGE THE PROMISE,
> AND THE LAW IS NOT GREATER THAN THE PROMISE.
> BUT THE LAW IS NOT CONTRARY TO THE PROMISE:
> THEY WORK TOGETHER TO BRING SINNERS TO THE SAVIOR."
>
> Warren Wiersbe – The Bible Exposition Commentary

DAY 1 – BEGIN IN PRAYER

1. Read Galatians 4.

2. Re-read Galatians 4:1-18.

3. What relationship does the believer in Christ have to God?

   How was this relationship formed?

4. What emotion do you see in Paul's writing as he strongly warns these believers in Galatia who are being seduced by false teachers?

5. What is the main point(s) that Paul is making in this portion of Galatians 4?

6. Your memory verse for this week is Galatians 4:6. Record it below and begin committing it to memory today.

DAY 2 – BEGIN IN PRAYER

1. Read Galatians 4:1-18.

2. Re-read Galatians 4:1-7.

3. Paul continues with another analogy to make sure we understand that salvation is not gained by the good works of man, but comes to us solely by God's grace working through our faith in the finished work of Jesus Christ at Calvary. This time he speaks of the child who is an heir and of the slave in his household. What is the same about the daily lives of these two individuals?

by GRACE, be Free

What does the figure of the child represent?

What does the figure of the adult son represent?

The word translated *child* in verse 1 means *an infant or a minor*, one who has not yet come to the age of maturity or adulthood. In Paul's culture the division between childhood and adulthood was much clearer than it is in our culture today. At an appointed time in the son's life a ceremony would take place and the child would be considered a man. From that day on, he was an adult with the full privileges of citizenship. In the Jewish culture that age was 13 and in the Greek culture it was 18. Therefore, Paul's readers would have easily related to his analogy. How does this truth relate to the subject of the Law and God's grace?

Review Galatians 3:23-29 to understand your position *as heirs according to the promise*. What is your position in Christ?

From your personal spiritual experience, what was it like the day you went from childhood to adulthood, from under the law, which brings conviction of sin, to grace that brings life?

4. One of the tragedies of legalism and works righteousness is that it makes a person appear to be a strong, mature believer when in reality they are firmly under the bondage of a system that does not produce life. Just as the human father sets a date for his son to become a man, so our Heavenly Father, *when the fullness of the time had come,* set a date for the Law to be fulfilled through the sending of His Son. Why did Jesus come? (v. 5)

What do the following Scriptures teach us about why God sent His Son to the world? How do these truths change your outlook today?

a. Isaiah 9:6, 7

b. Micah 5:2

c. Luke 2:10,11

d. John 1:14

e. 1John 4:9, 10

5. In God's perfect timing He sent His Son, completely man (born of a woman) and completely God. According to verse 5, God sent His Son to *redeem those who were under the law.* Use your dictionary of Bible words to define the following words.

Redeem (v. 5)

Adoption (v. 5)

Once we came to understand, through the tutorship of the law, that we were sinners in need of a Savior, then we were willing to surrender our lives to Jesus Christ. He redeemed us, bought us back, as a slave is bought from the auction block and set free. With this redemption, we are adopted as sons. What benefits of this new family relationship are detailed for us in verses 6 and 7?

The New Testament word for *adoption* means *to place as an adult son.* It has to do with our standing in the family of God: we are not little children but adult sons with all of the privileges of sonship. He has given us His Spirit dwelling in our hearts, which provides us intimate access to our Heavenly Father, and we are no longer slaves. What insight do you gain from the following Scriptures about the indwelling Holy Spirit and this family relationship?

a. Romans 8:16, 17

b. 2Corinthians 1:20-22

c. Ephesians 4:30

d. Hebrews 4:15, 16

6. What specific lesson(s) did you learn from today's study and how will it make a difference in how you live this week?

7. Continue to work on memorizing Galatians 4:6 for this week. Be careful not to neglect this important part of the study.

DAY 3 – BEGIN IN PRAYER

1. Read Galatians 4:1-18.

2. Re-read Galatians 4:8-11.

3. Prior to the grace found in Jesus, the Galatians had served gods that were not gods at all. They did so out of ignorance. Now, they were departing from grace and returning to a system of works that could not save, nor could it bring them closer to God. Can you relate to Paul's fear and concern for these believers?

Have you ever had this deep of a concern for someone in your life who was turning away from the truth to follow a lie? What is our responsibility towards this person?

a. Galatians 6:1, 2

b. 1Thessalonians 5:14

c. Jude 1:22, 23

d. James 5:19, 20

4. The phrase *weak and beggarly* elements gives us an idea of the extent of the regression in faith that was happening in the hearts of these believers. They were giving up the power and wealth of the Gospel for the weakness and poverty of the Law, and some were returning to the ritualistic observance of days, months, seasons and years. What warning did Paul give to the Colossian church in Colossians 2:16, 17 that would be applicable to these believers as well?

    What kinds of elementary rules and regulations could a straying believer wrongly place himself in bondage to today?

    How is this warning applicable in your walk with the Lord?

    If we turn from grace and begin to rely upon our works to please God, what sacrificial act are we neglecting that took us from the depths of sin to saving grace?

5. Do you think that these verses in Galatians mean that it is wrong for the Christian to celebrate special days of observance? Why, or why not?

    What is to be the motive of the believer's heart in these special days of celebration?

According to Romans 14:4-13, what is our responsibility toward our brethren when it comes to days and methods by which we/they worship the Lord?

What emotion do you think is behind Paul's words in Galatians 4:11?

What similar plea did he make to the Corinthian church in 2Corinthians 11:2, 3?

6. What specific lesson(s) did you learn from today's study and how will it make a difference in how you live this week?

7. Continue to work on memorizing Galatians 4:6 for this week. Can you record it below without looking?

DAY 4 – BEGIN IN PRAYER

1. Read Galatians 4:1-18.

2. Re-read Galatians 4:12-16.

3. In these next verses we see Paul change his tone and tactics. He leaves the doctrinal and Scriptural evidence and begins to speak to the church with a heartfelt appeal. What passionate plea does he make in verse 12?

There is a gentleness in Paul's words that is an absolute necessity in the life of every believer. We are never to become hardened to the plight of the unbeliever or insensitive to those who struggle with obedience and sin. Even though we cannot compromise the truth of the Gospel, we must defend it in love. What do the following Scriptures teach us about this truth?

a. Romans 12:6-10

b. Ephesians 4:14-16

c. 1Peter 1:22

What do you think Paul meant when he urged the Galatian believers to become like him?

How had Paul become like them?

4.   How had these believers received Paul when he came into their cities?

Such acceptance in this ancient culture was a miracle in itself. It seems that Paul was sick and not a pretty sight to behold, and yet they received him, and they eagerly received the Word of God and Jesus Christ as Lord. They loved him and were willing to sacrifice almost anything for him. How might this acceptance be explained by the following verses?

a. Luke 10:16

b. John 13:20

c. 1Thessalonians 4:8

Personal: Do you find any comfort from these truths when those you love do not receive your witness?

5. Nothing tears the heart of a faithful pastor, teacher, youth leader or missionary more than seeing someone they have led to the Lord walk away from Him and into the deception of the enemy and the world. Even then, what is the heart of the Lord toward these who walk in rebellion according to Matthew 23:37?

In Paul's plea we see the heart of the Father as He longs for the love and repentance of His children. He calls them to Himself like the father who waits for His prodigal son. What is Paul's question to those he loves in verse 16?

Read the parable of the prodigal son in Luke 15:11-32, what was the Father doing while the son was away?

What promise of forgiveness is given in 1John 1:9 to those who come to the Lord with a fully repentant heart?

Personal: Has your heart been broken because someone has walked away from Jesus? Will you make a commitment today to do the very best you can for them by daily interceding for them at the throne of grace?

6. What specific lesson(s) did you learn from today's study and how will it make a difference in how you live this week?

7. Continue to work on memorizing Galatians 4:6 for this week. How are you doing?

DAY 5 – BEGIN IN PRAYER

1. Read Galatians 4:1-18. (No skipping this!)

2. Re-read Galatians 4:17-18.

3. The false teachers were zealously courting these Galatian believers. They were acting as if they cared for them, but their true intentions were to shut the Galatians out of God's grace, and gain instead, recognition and support for their false teachings. In contrast, the true godly spiritual leader is interested in the good of the individual, their growth, health and spiritual progress. What warnings are we given that will protect us from falling into the trap of these false teachers?

    a. 2Corinthians 11:13-15

    b. 2Peter 2:1-3

    c. 2Peter 2:18-20

4. It was not the zealousness that Paul was opposed to, but the motives behind the zealousness. Today cults and their false teachers zealously court followers, but they do so, in order to gain from them. They do not do so for the good of those who follow them. How does Romans 16:17, 18 describe these leaders?

    What instruction are we given in the above passage of Scripture that will protect us from straying from the truth of the Gospel?

    These Judaizers had no interest in the Galatian believers beyond trapping them in legalism. What stern rebuke did Jesus give to those who had these same corrupt motives in Matthew 23:15?

5. Paul reminds us that there is a zealousness that is a good thing. He was zealous toward them in preaching the Gospel when he first came to the Galatia region. We are to be zealous in winning souls to Christ, because He is the very best gift we can give. What is our work ethic to be like as we daily serve the Lord and share the Good News of salvation?

    a. 1Corinthians 15:58

    b. Galatians 6:9, 10

    c. Colossians 2:6, 7

    d. Colossians 3:23, 24

6. What specific lesson(s) did you learn from today's study and how will it make a difference in how you live this week?

7. Continue to work on memorizing Galatians 4:6 for this week.

DAY 6 – BEGIN IN PRAYER

1. Read Galatians 4.

2. Re-read Galatians 4:1-18.

3. How would you summarize the truth taught in verses 1-18?

4. What truth has made a difference in your walk with the Lord this week?

5. Can you record Galatians 4:6 in the space below without looking at it? If not, continue to work on it today until you can.

DAY 1 – BEGIN IN PRAYER

1. Read Galatians 4.

2. Re-read Galatians 4:19-31.

3. What sad observation does Paul make about those who had trusted him and faithfully followed the Lord Jesus Christ? (vs. 19-20)

4. In these final verses of chapter 4 Paul contrasts grace and the law, or faith verses works, by using an Old Testament story as the analogy and an illustration of the grace of God. What does Mt. Sinai and Hagar, the bondwoman, represent?

   What does Isaac, the son born of the freewoman, represent?

5. What is the main point(s) that Paul is making in this last portion of Galatians 4? How does it specifically apply to your walk with the Lord Jesus Christ today?

6. Your memory verse for this week is Galatians 4:31. Record it below and begin committing it to memory today.

DAY 2 – BEGIN IN PRAYER

1. Read Galatians 4:19-31.

2. We are doing a bit of backtracking today to explore Paul's analogy and illustration. Read the following portions of Genesis and record a few key details to help you remember the story.

by Grace, *be* Free

a. Genesis 15:1-6

b. Genesis 16

c. Genesis 17

d. Genesis 18:1-14

e. Genesis 21:1-21

3.   Using the details of this Genesis account can you explain why Paul was feeling such heartbreak over those who had come to faith in Jesus Christ and were now choosing to return to the bondage of the law?

4.   How does the truth in this account in Genesis apply to how you walk in grace, by faith, today?

5.   Continue to work on memorizing Galatians 4:31 for this week. Be careful not to neglect this important part of the study.

DAY 3 – BEGIN IN PRAYER

1. Read Galatians 4:19-31.

2. Re-read Galatians 4:19-20.

3. As a mother would speak to a child, Paul continues to try to persuade his wayward children of the error of their way. What unnatural pain was Paul suffering because of their bad choices?

    What does 1 Thessalonians 2:7-8 teach us about the concern that Paul had for his fellow brethren?

4. Paul had labored in the process of bringing his *little children* to life in Christ Jesus and sadly, now he was suffering the same labor pains again. These abnormal pains were accompanied by severe heartbreak. Paul was desperately trying to keep them from falling back into legalism. No matter how painful the heartbreak, Paul would not forsake these wayward believers *until Christ was formed in them*. What lesson can we learn from his persistent love that will assist us in dealing with the wayward ones in our lives?

    Last week we studied a series of Scriptures that outlined our responsibility toward our wayward brethren. Review these instructions, thinking specifically about the people in your life who may be breaking your heart by going astray.

    a. Galatians 6:1, 2

    b. 1 Thessalonians 5:14

    c. Jude 1:22, 23

    d. James 5:19, 20

Spend a few moments in prayer for those who are being drawn away from the truth of the Gospel. This is our very best offensive tool!

5. Paul declares, *I have doubts about you*. Use a Dictionary of Bible Words or other resource to define the word translated doubts in verse 20.

Paul didn't know what else he could do. If he had been with them he may have resorted to grabbing their shoulders and trying to shake some sense into them. What do we learn about the heart of the Shepherd toward the straying sheep from Matthew 18:12-14?

What clear direction and application are we given in Matthew 18:15-17 to guide us in the restoration of a brother or sister who falls into sin?

Selah: Are we given freedom to discuss their sin with anyone other than those mentioned in the above verses? Beware of the enemy's tactics to divide and destroy the Body of Christ through gossip!

6. What specific lesson(s) did you learn from today's study and how will it make a difference in how you live this week?

7. Continue to work on memorizing Galatians 4:31 for this week.

DAY 4 – BEGIN IN PRAYER

1. Read Galatians 4:19-31.

2. Read Galatians 4:21-27.

3. Paul's question to his readers is this, do you really understand what the law requires of you? He begins by saying, let me use an allegory to explain. From our study on day two, what was God's plan for the descendents of Abraham?

    When and how did the plan go wrong?

    What did you learn about the two sons of Abraham?

    What severe action did the LORD require of Abraham regarding his son who was born according to the flesh?

4. The spiritual application for the believers in Galatia, and for us today, is that the Law does not bring life. Paul tells us that he is speaking of two covenants – one given from Mount Sinai. According to verse 24, what is the result of this covenant?

    God gave the Old Testament law to Moses at Mt. Sinai. It was a law that was impossible to keep and it symbolizes Hagar and the earthly Jerusalem. These are representative of people trying to make their way to heaven based on their own righteousness. Ishmael represents the work of the flesh. God did not ask for nor did He require Abraham, Sarah, and Hagar's works of the flesh. What He wanted was their obedience! What He wanted was their faith and trust in His clear, spoken word. Since it can't be repeated too often, because we daily face the temptation to rely on our own strength and good works, what does the Word teach us about the Law?

    a. Acts 13:38, 39

b. Romans 3:20

c. Romans 3:28

d. Galatians 3:11-14

5. By comparison, Sarah, Isaac, and the Jerusalem from above speak of faith and grace. With the finished work of Jesus Christ at Calvary that which had been barren, waiting for the Messiah, could now bear much fruit by grace through faith. What promise do you have regarding His grace in your life today?

a. Ephesians 2:8-10

b. Philippians 3:8, 9

c. Titus 3:5-7

d. Hebrews 4:16

Personal: Are there ways that you are tempted to fall back upon good works that do not produce true righteousness? What can you do today that will help you to remember that the work is complete and the price is paid in full?

Challenge: What is the difference between works of the Law (by which no man is justified) and the good works that are the fruit of a transformed, born-again life?

6. What specific lesson(s) did you learn from today's study and how will it make a difference in how you live this week?

7. Continue to work on memorizing Galatians 4:31 for this week.

DAY 5 – BEGIN IN PRAYER

1. Read Galatians 4:19-31.

2. Re-read Galatians 4:28-31.

3. Paul challenges us to apply these truths personally. As believers, we are children of faith and it is not too surprising that the children of the flesh will persecute us by the law and by self-effort, even as Ishmael mocked Isaac. When the question of legalism arises, there will always be a temptation to return to the place from which we were set free. Why do you think that the one who holds to salvation by works, trusting in their own performance of the law, would persecute the one walking in freedom by grace?

    What promise do you have if you suffer such persecution?

    a. John 16:33

    b. Romans 5:1-5

    c. Romans 8:35-39

    d. Revelation 2:9, 10

4. When we take Paul's allegory and apply it to our lives spiritually, what must be cast out of our lives, as Hagar and Ishmael were sent away by Abraham?

    How do you think this command of the LORD affected Abraham as he willingly obeyed?

    Do you think it was easy? Do you think it was painful? Why was it necessary?

    What are we to do with those works of the flesh that plague us and keep us from walking in the Spirit by grace?

    a. Romans 6:6-13

    b. Galatians 5:24

5. According to verse 30, what promise is given to the children of the freewoman that will not be received by the sons of the bondwoman?

    So then brethren, consider who you are! What is your inheritance?

    Add these to your list if you hadn't already! How do these truths change the way you walk today?

    a. Romans 5:9-10

    b. Romans 8:15-17

c. Ephesians 1:17-19

d. 1Peter 1:3-5

6. What specific lesson(s) did you learn from today's study and how will it make a difference in how you live this week?

7. Continue to work on memorizing Galatians 4:31 for this week.

DAY 6 – BEGIN IN PRAYER

1. Read Galatians 4.

2. Re-read Galatians 4:19-31.

3. How would you summarize the truth taught in verses 19-31?

4. What truth has made a difference in your walk with the Lord this week?

5. Can you record Galatians 4:31 in the space below without looking at it? If not, continue to work on it today until you can.

Book Recommendation:
If you have never read Pastor Chuck Smith's Book
"Why Grace Changes Everything", it is a must read!
If you have read it but it has been awhile, it's probably time to read it again!

82

DAY 1 – BEGIN IN PRAYER

1.   Read Galatians 5.

2.   Re-read Galatians 5:1-15.

3.   What is the main subject of each of the following portions of this week's lesson?

Verses 1-4

Verses 5-9

Verses 10-12

Verses 13-15

4.   What do you learn about Christian liberty from Galatians 5:1-15?

How are we to correctly use our Christian liberty?

5.   What verse or verses speak to your heart today? Why?

6.   Your memory verse for this week is Galatians 5:1. Record it below and begin committing it to memory today.

DAY 2 – BEGIN IN PRAYER

1. Read Galatians 5:1-15.

2. Read Galatians 5:1-4.

3. Paul begins a new section in his letter to the churches of Galatia. He has written about his experience with grace (chapters 1-2) and given us a very precise teaching on the doctrine of grace (chapters 3-4). Now he turns from theory to application, from doctrine to practice. True faith is more than believing the truth; it is bearing fruit in the daily practice of our lives. Right doctrine should result in right living. What strong exhortation do we find in Galatians 5:1?

    What is the positive action that we must take as believers?

    What negative pressure are we to resist?

    Why is the person who practices a religion of **works of righteousness** in which they must keep a certain code of rules and regulations trapped **with a yoke of bondage?**

    What more do we learn from Peter's discussion of the yoke of bondage in Acts 15:7-11?

4. Paul proceeds to give us four practical observations and the dangers that await those who would go back to the bondage of the law from which they had been set free. The first is found in verse 2, what is it?

    If these believers returned to the practice of the law (the clear outward sign of the law was the rite of circumcision), the finished work of Christ at Calvary would be of no benefit to them. It cannot be Jesus Christ **and** anything else. Salvation is extended to the believer by grace through faith in Jesus Christ alone! How do the following Scriptures from the Book of Romans support this truth?

a. Romans 9:30-33

b. Romans 10:1-4

5.   In verse 3 Paul gives us the second danger that awaits those who would go back to the bondage of the law. What is required of them?

The demand of righteousness by the law is 100% perfection in both action and intent. Therefore, the one who falls back into legalism to attain righteousness has no room for error. How do the following Scriptures speak to this truth?

a. Deuteronomy 27:26

b. Galatians 3:10

c. James 2:10-11

d. Matthew 5:21-22; 27-28; 30

According to verse 4, what is the third danger for those *who attempt to be justified by law?*

Use a Dictionary of New Testament Words or other Biblical resource to define the word translated *estranged* (NKJV) in verse 4.

6.   What specific lesson(s) did you learn from today's study and how will it make a difference in how you live this week?

7.   Continue to work on memorizing Galatians 5:1 for this week. Be careful not to neglect this important part of the study.

DAY 3 – BEGIN IN PRAYER

1.   Read Galatians 5:1-15.

2.   Re-read Galatians 5:5-9.

3.   Yesterday we learned of three of the four dangers of turning from grace to the law. The fourth danger, or the end result, of trying to be righteous by the law is that we exclude ourselves from right standing with God. According to verse 5, how do we obtain righteousness?

Use a Dictionary of New Testament Words or other Biblical resource to define the word translated *righteousness* (NKJV) in verse 5.

What do we learn from the Book of Romans regarding the righteousness that comes through faith?

a. Romans 3:21-26

b. Romans 5:17-21

c. Romans 10:8-11

4. As believers in Jesus Christ we have been made righteous through Him. How does Ephesians 1:3-6 change your outlook on life today?

    Paul tells us that it is through the Spirit that we are to eagerly wait for the hope of righteousness by faith. We already possess the *imputed* righteousness of *justification* that comes by faith (Ephesians 1:4). However, our yet incomplete righteousness of *sanctification and glorification* still awaits us. It is not the outward keeping of the law or rules and regulations that avails anything – it is our faith working through love. What then is to be the motive for *everything* we do?

    What do you learn from these references that encourages you to serve out of love and keeps you from falling into the trap of legalism?

    a. John 3:16, 17

    b. 1John 4:9, 10

    c. 1John 4:19

    d. Romans 13:8-10

5. Paul turns from speaking about the dangers of the false doctrine that was threatening this body of believers at Galatia to address the character of the men who were teaching the false doctrine. This body of believers <u>had</u> run well. Like the marathon runner in the Olympics, they had been on track, growing and making progress when something tragic happened. According to the question in verse 7, what took place that stopped their forward progress?

    What does verse 8 tell us about *this persuasion?*

What did Paul say about *this persuasion* in the opening of this letter (Galatians 1:6, 7)?

What does Paul mean when he says, *a little leaven leavens the whole lump?*

What do these verses add to your understanding of the concept of leaven in the Bible?

a. Matthew 16:6-12

b. 1Corinthians 5:6, 7

6.   What specific lesson(s) did you learn from today's study and how will it make a difference in how you live this week?

7.   Continue to work on memorizing Galatians 5:1 for this week.

DAY 4 – BEGIN IN PRAYER

1.   Read Galatians 5:1-15.

2.   Re-read Galatians 5:10-12.

3.   We have learned that the false teachers in the Galatian church, and those who attack the church today, can be identified in that they hinder the truth (v. 7), they do not come from God (v. 8) and they have a major contaminating influence in the church, spreading their lies among the true believers and those who need to find Jesus. What destiny awaits these false teachers (v. 10)?

What does Jesus declare in Matthew 18:6, 7 about those who would cause a brother to sin?

What does 2Peter 2:1-3 & 9 add that stands as a severe warning to any who teach false doctrine?

What is our responsibility as brethren to protect one another?

a. Romans 14:13-15

b. Romans 15:1, 2

c. 1Corinthians 8:9-12

4.   The fourth characteristic of false teachers is that they will bear their own judgment. As for the believer who gets caught up in their lies, they will lose their peace, joy and rest. But, we can have confidence, along with Paul, that the Lord will keep His children safely until the end. They may momentarily drift off the straight path but the Good Shepherd will bring them back. What do you learn from the following Scriptures that bring you rest in your walk today?

a. John 10:4-5, 14

b. John 10:27-29

5.   Historically, false religion has been the most effective tool of Satan in his battle with God and His people. What is the fifth characteristic of the false teacher found in verse 11?

If Paul continued to preach circumcision, or salvation by works, how would things in his life be different?

What is the *offense* to those who would lead people away from grace (v. 11)?

What do you learn about the choice each of us must make?

a. 1 Corinthians 1:18

b. 1 Corinthians 1:23, 24

c. 1 Peter 2:7, 8

In verse 12 we read one of Paul's harshest recorded statements. In the New American Standard Version it reads, *would that those who are troubling you would even mutilate themselves*. If they longed to submit themselves to the Law, maybe he was suggesting that they follow another pagan practice that promulgated castration. Can you relate to his indignation when you see those you love being deceived? What is your most powerful offensive weapon? Are you using it without ceasing?

6. What specific lesson(s) did you learn from today's study and how will it make a difference in how you live this week?

7. Continue to work on memorizing Galatians 5:1 for this week.

DAY 5 – BEGIN IN PRAYER

1. Read Galatians 5:1-15.

2. Re-read Galatians 5:13-15.

3. There is much debate in the church about liberty or freedom and it usually centers on the freedom of man to pursue his wishes and wants. The truth is, man apart from God is not free, rather he is bound to sin and the flesh, and to self and death. What very clear direction are we given in verse 13 regarding our liberty, and how we are to practice it in our daily walk with the Lord?

    What do the following Scriptures add to the subject of your freedoms and how you are to use them?

    a. Romans 6:18-22

    b. 1 Peter 2:15, 16

    c. 1 Corinthians 8:9

    Practically speaking, how does this affect your daily walk? What do you have the freedom to do that in doing so might hurt someone else's walk? Are you willing to forgo your freedom to *through love serve one another?*

4. As believers we are finally given true freedom to do what we could never do before. We can do what God wants, expects and longs for from us. We have been given the indwelling Holy Spirit that enables us to obey His commands. This is true liberty! What command is the fulfillment of all the law?

    How many references can you find that instruct you *to love one another?* List them by book and chapter.

    Write out your favorite on a separate paper and carry it with you today!

    What further instructions are we given about our relationship to others in the following Scriptures?

a. Ephesians 4:31, 32

b. 1 Peter 3:8, 9

5. Sadly, it is far too common that we practice the very opposite of loving one another in the church today. What warning are we given in verse 15 that should bring us to repentance when we choose to walk in the flesh?

    If we choose to judge, condemn and command that others walk, look and talk like us, the end result will be destruction. It will be the destruction of our fellowship, the destruction of our relationship, and the destruction of our witness to the world. Just think about it, every time we put someone down, make a snide remark, roll our eyes, or whisper behind their back...sooner or later we will be hurt to the same degree. How will the following Scriptures help you to walk in love today?

    a. Matthew 7:1, 2

    b. Mark 4:21-23

    c. James 2:13

6. What specific lesson(s) did you learn from today's study and how will it make a difference in how you live this week?

7. Continue to work on memorizing Galatians 5:1 for this week.

DAY 6 – BEGIN IN PRAYER

1. Read Galatians 5.

2. Re-read Galatians 5:1-15.

3. How would you summarize the truth taught in verses 1-15?

4. What truth has made a difference in your walk with the Lord this week?

5. Can you record Galatians 5:1 in the space below without looking at it? If not, continue to work on it today until you can.

94

DAY 1 ~ BEGIN IN PRAYER

1.   Read Galatians 5.

2.   Re-read Galatians 5:16-26.

3.   What is the main subject of each of the following portions of this week's lesson?

Verses 16-18

Verses 19-21

Verses 22-23

Verses 24-26

4.   How can we be certain that we will not be drawn into the temptation of the lust of the flesh?

5.   What is the clear sign that a person truly belongs to Christ (v. 24)?

6.   Your memory verse for this week is Galatians 5:16. Record it below and begin committing it to memory today.

DAY 2 ~ BEGIN IN PRAYER

1.   Read Galatians 5:16-26.

2.   Re-read Galatians 5:16-18.

3. Since it is clear that we have been saved by grace, Paul encourages us to continue in that grace by walking according to the Holy Spirit that dwells in us. What do you think it means when we are instructed to *walk in the Spirit?*

    How do the following Scriptures help you define what it means to walk in the Spirit?

    a. Romans 8:1-6

    b. Romans 8:12-16

    c. Colossians 3:5-10

    d. Titus 3:3-8

4. The word *walk* in Galatians 5:16 is *peripateo* in Greek. It is in the present tense, meaning a regular on-going action, and it is in the imperative mood, which means it is not a suggestion, but a command. The good news is we have His Spirit, which empowers us to overcome the flesh. It is a choice we must make moment-by-moment and day-by-day. What promise do we find in Philippians 2:12, 13?

    Personal: What choices have you already had to make today in regards to obeying the Spirit or surrendering to the flesh? Could you have done better? Will you make it your prayer today?

5. The awesome thing about being born again is that the Holy Spirit has come to dwell within us. His role is to lead us, teach us, guide and direct us, and

to strengthen and enable us in our walk with Jesus. We who were once dead in sin have been made alive (born again) and it is the indwelling Holy Spirit that empowers us *to walk in the Spirit*. What enemy will we **always** have to contend with while we are in this body (v.17)?

Read about the Apostle Paul's struggle in Romans 7:18-25. According to verse 25, why can we have great assurance of victory?

Paul gives us a clear injunction (v. 16) and then reminds us that we will always face a battle (v. 17). What solution is given in verse 18?

It is great news that victory over the flesh is not in keeping the Law or in seeking by our own ability to do what is right because both are futile. What we are called to do is to submit to the leading of the Spirit. Our focus is not to be on the flesh, but on the Spirit. The Holy Spirit dwells in you, you are not under the Law – you are FREE! How does the truth of Galatians 4:4-7 change your outlook on today?

6. What specific lesson(s) did you learn from today's study and how will it make a difference in how you live this week?

7. Continue to work on memorizing Galatians 5:16 for this week. Be careful not to neglect this important part of the study.

DAY 3 – BEGIN IN PRAYER

1. Read Galatians 5:16-26.

2. Re-read Galatians 5:19-21.

3. Paul gives us some definable and very recognizable characteristics of a life lived by, or in, the flesh. He declares, *the works of the flesh are evident*...Use an English Language dictionary to define the following works of the flesh:

   Adultery

   Fornication

   Uncleanness (Unclean)

   Lewdness

   Idolatry

   Sorcery

   Hatred

   Contentions

   Jealousy

   Wrath

   Selfish ambitions

   Dissention

Heresies

Envy

Murder

Drunkenness

Revelries

4. Do you think Paul has made a complete list of all the works of the flesh? Why or why not?

5. What very clear declaration is made in verse 21 about those who **practice** such a sinful lifestyle?

Before we end this day's study I think we are in need of some good news. What does 1 Corinthians 6:9-11 (especially 11) say to encourage your heart?

6. What specific lesson(s) did you learn from today's study and how will it make a difference in how you live this week?

7. Continue to work on memorizing Galatians 5:16 for this week. Can you record it without looking yet?

DAY 4 ~ BEGIN IN PRAYER

1. Read Galatians 5:16-26.

2.   Re-read Galatians 5:22-23.

3.   The works of the flesh are the result of the old nature of sin and darkness, and they are controlled by self-will and self-effort. In contrast, the <u>fruit</u> of the Spirit is that which God Himself produces in the lives of those who have surrendered their hearts to Him as fertile ground. We are told the fruit (not fruits) of the Spirit is love – as defined by the rest of the list. What is the definition of love according to verse 22?

4.   How is love defined in John 3:16, 17?

     What does Romans 5:8-10 say about this amazing love?

     What direction are we given in John 13:34, 35 and what will be the result of this love in our lives?

5.   What do you learn about each of these characteristics of love from the following references?

     a. John 15:9-11

     b. John 14:27

     c. 2Peter 3:9

d. Titus 3:4-6

e. Romans 2:4

f. Psalm 89:1-4

Paul brings up the concept *of the law* again in 5:23. What is his point to the legalistic Galatians?

(Hint: can following the Law produce this fruit or can the Law in any way condemn this fruit?)

6.   What specific lesson(s) did you learn from today's study and how will it make a difference in how you live this week?

7.   Continue to work on memorizing Galatians 5:16 for this week. Can you record it without looking?

DAY 5 – BEGIN IN PRAYER

1.   Read Galatians 5:16-26.

2.   Re-read Galatians 5:24-26.

3.   What is the believer to do about the ongoing conflict between the flesh and the Spirit that we face daily?

What does it mean to have *crucified the flesh?*

What does Romans 6:6-8 teach about the process?

According to Romans 6:11-14, what is our responsibility in this work that was completed on the cross at Calvary?

Personal: As believers, we have the freedom to choose not to sin – this is not possible for those in the world, because they are under the bondage of sin. The question lies in the decision – are you choosing to die daily to your flesh or are you more often choosing to walk in the flesh? Re-read Galatians 5:24.

4. Paul used this word *crucified* two other times in his letter to the Galatians. What did he say and how does believing and doing it make a difference in your life today?

    a. Galatians 2:20

    b. Galatians 6:14

What does it mean to *live in the Spirit and walk in the Spirit?*

How does Romans 8:1-6 help you to understand how we are to live and walk in the Spirit?

Practically speaking, what might it mean for you today *to walk in the Spirit?*

Give a recent personal example of something you did at the leading of the Holy Spirit?

5. According to verses 25-26, what is the connection between our walk in the Spirit and our relationship with one another?

What further instruction do we find in the following verses about how walking in the Spirit will change and improve our personal relationships?

a. Romans 12:10

b. 1Corinthians 10:23, 24

c. Philippians 2:1-3

d. 1Peter 5:5

6. What specific lesson(s) did you learn from today's study and how will it make a difference in how you live this week?

7. Continue to work on memorizing Galatians 5:16 for this week. Can you record it without looking yet?

DAY 6 – BEGIN IN PRAYER

1. Read Galatians 5. (No Fair Skipping this – it's important!)

2. Re-read Galatians 5:16-26.

3.   How would you summarize the truth taught in verses 16-26?

4.   What truth has made a difference in your walk with the Lord this week?

5.   Can you record Galatians 5:16 in the space below without looking at it? If not, continue to work on it today until you can.

DAY 1 – BEGIN IN PRAYER

1. Read Galatians 6.

2. Re-read Galatians 6-1-18.

3. What is the main subject of each of the following portions of this week's lesson?

    Verses 1-5

    Verses 6-10

    Verses 11-13

    Verses 14-18

4. According to Galatians 6, what responsibility do we have to a wayward brother or sister?

5. What encouragement do you find from Paul's final words to the church at Galatia?

    What warnings do we find in this chapter that should keep us from straying from the path of righteousness?

6. Your memory verse for this week is Galatians 6:7, 8. Record it below and begin committing it to memory today.

DAY 2 – BEGIN IN PRAYER

1. Read Galatians 6. (The whole thing! You can do it!)

2. Read Galatians 6:1-5.

3. With the clear description of the fruit of the Spirit in mind Paul continues by reminding us of our obligation to watch after and protect one another to the best of our ability. What instruction are we given in verses 1 and 2?

    Who is to restore?

    How are they to do so?

    What warning is given to the believer who seeks to restore his/her brethren?

    Why do you think such a warning is necessary? (Galatians 6:3)

    What do the following Scriptures add that helps us to understand our responsibility to love, serve and protect one another?

    a. James 5:19, 20

    b. Jude 1:22, 23

4. Those who live in the grace of the Holy Spirit see themselves as sinful and weak. They rely on grace themselves so it is only a natural outcome of the Spirit that they deal with others in the same grace. Use a Bible Dictionary to define the following words to better understand their meaning:

    a. Overtaken (v. 1)

b. Restore (v. 1)

c. Bear (v. 2)

d. Examine (v. 4)

5.   As believers we are *to bear one another's burdens*, what does verse 2 teach us about this awesome act of love?

According to verses 3 and 4, what character trait is clearly evident in the one who is willing to love others as Galatians 5:22, 23 describes?

We must be careful not to think that we have "arrived" and look down on those who have been *overtaken in a trespass* thinking that we are above failing. What stern warning is given in 1 Corinthians 10:12, 13 that will protect us from sin?

While we are responsible to help others who have fallen to find healing and restoration, what direction we are given in verses 4 and 5? Who is ultimately responsible for our daily walk with the Lord?

In verse 2 the word translated *burden* speaks of a heavy weight. The word translated *load* in verse 5 refers to anything that is carried, and has no connotation of difficulty. It is often used of the general obligations of life that a person is responsible to bear on his own. Therefore, we all must carry our **own** load and not always rely on others for their help. We are to stand on our own feet in the strength of the Lord, becoming mature and complete in our faith. When we see someone fall, all of us are to run to their aid so that they might be restored. However, we all must stand individually before the Lord and give an account for the life we have lived. How will the following Scriptures affect your choices today?

a. Romans 14:10-12

b. 2Corinthians 5:10

c. 1Corinthians 3:12-15

6.   What specific lesson(s) did you learn from today's study and how will it make a difference in how you live this week?

7.   Continue to work on memorizing Galatians 6:7, 8 for this week. Be careful not to neglect this important part of the study.

DAY 3 – BEGIN IN PRAYER

1.   Read Galatians 6.

2.   Re-read Galatians 6:6-10.

3.   What are we taught about giving and receiving in these verses?

What instruction is given to those who are taught the Word?

What more can we learn about the privilege and duty of giving to our home fellowship and the Christian ministries that strengthen and build up our faith?

a. Deuteronomy 12:19

b. 1 Corinthians 9:9-14

c. 1 Timothy 5:17, 18

4. The word translated *share or communicate* in verse 6 means *to hold in common*. The word in Greek is *koinonia* and speaks of fellowship – fellowship in Jesus Christ and fellowship with one another. From the very beginning of the church, sharing was one of the marks of the Christian experience. Paul turns our attention to the eternal law of reaping and sowing. What promise, with warning, is given to us in verses 7 and 8?

Whatever the farmer **plants** – the farmer **reaps**. If he sows beans, he reaps beans. He does not sow beans and reap apple trees! In like manner, spiritually speaking, whatever the believer sows – the believer reaps. If we sow to the flesh we will reap corruption! It is a guarantee! Review Galatians 5:19-21 for the outcome of sowing to the flesh. What does Galatians 5:21 say about those who practice such things?

Practically speaking, how are we to sow to the Spirit?

How do the following Scriptures support your answer?

a. Deuteronomy 15:7-10

b. Proverbs 22:9

c. 2Corinthians 9:6-8

d. 1Peter 4:9, 10

e. Romans 12:6-11

5.   The sowing and reaping process requires patient waiting. The fruit is not evident overnight! What promise are we given in verse 9 that will certainly sustain us in the waiting process?

Read and mediate on the following Scriptures – how do they encourage you today?

a. 2Corinthians 4:16-18

b. Hebrews 10:35-37

c. James 5:7, 8

Personal: Are you weary in well doing? The cure is to lay your burdens at Jesus' feet in prayer and turn your focus to the promised harvest rather than the daily circumstances!

We are told that, *as we have opportunity, let us do good to all, especially to those who are of the household of faith.* Why do you think we often miss opportunities that the Lord has laid before us? What can you do to keep from missing these valuable opportunities?

6. What specific lesson(s) did you learn from today's study and how will it make a difference in how you live this week?

7. Continue to work on memorizing Galatians 6:7, 8 for this week.

DAY 4 – BEGIN IN PRAYER

1. Read Galatians 6.

2. Read Galatians 6:11-13.

3. Most of Paul's letters were dictated by him but written by another because he had very bad eyes and could hardly see to write. Therefore, he mentions the large letters he used to write this letter himself. As he signs off this awesome epistle about grace, he gives us one final contrast asking his readers whether they serve for the praises of men or the praises of God. In these last few verses, Paul is dealing with *motive*. The question is *why* do we do what we do? What were the *motives* of the Judiazers in Galatia that caused them to seek to draw the believers back under the Law?

How did Jesus describe the "religious leaders" who served for the wrong reasons and what stern warning with eternal consequences was given to them and anyone who would follow in their footsteps?

a. Matthew 6:2, 5, 7

b. Matthew 23:13-15

c. Luke 18:9-14

4. The Judiazer desired to make a good showing in the flesh by compelling those who were walking in grace to be circumcised. According to verse 12, what was one of their reasons for doing so?

The cross of Christ has always been an offense to the religion of works. The cross stands for the finished work of Christ at Calvary, and it points to grace – not works. What does 1Corinthians 1:23, 24 add to your understanding of the power of the cross?

Paul speaks of the cowardice behind the motives of the Judiazers. They identified themselves with the church but not with **the cross**, and therefore **not with Christ.** They did this to avoid persecution. What promises are given to all those who truly embrace the cross of Christ?

a. Matthew 5:10-12

b. John 15:19-21

c. 2Timothy 3:12

d. 1Peter 4:12-14

5. According to verse 13, what was another reason the Judiazers desired to have the Galatians drawn back to the Law of circumcision?

Were these Judiazers able to fully obey the high standards of the Mosaic Law?

Review the purpose of the Law according to Galatians 3:21-25. Why was the Law given?

Personal: The question to each of us is: why do you do what you do when it comes to serving the Lord? A good work is spoiled by a bad motive. Spend some time today thinking about why you do what you do – is it for the praises of men or the praises of God?

6. What specific lesson(s) did you learn from today's study and how will it make a difference in how you live this week?

7. Continue to work on memorizing Galatians 6:7, 8 for this week.

DAY 5 – BEGIN IN PRAYER

1. Read Galatians 6.

2. Re-read Galatians 6:14-18.

3. The Judiazers sought to gain converts so that they could boast in the flesh – or put another notch in their belt! What does Paul declare is the **only** thing that he could boast in?

   According to Philippians 3:7-8, what attitude did Paul take toward any prior accomplishment?

   What was the true desire of his heart and the goal for his life according to Philippians 3:9-10?

Review the following verses from Galatians. Do they accurately reflect the direction and goal of your heart and life?

a. Galatians 2:20

b. Galatians 5:24

4. Our only glory is that Jesus died on a cross for our sins and in so doing delivered us from this world system of works righteousness. We are to glory in Jesus, not denominations, baptisms, worship on certain days, or what is acceptable to eat on which day! We are to glory in Jesus and Jesus only! How do the following Scriptures help you to better focus on pleasing God and not men?

a. Jeremiah 9:24

b. 1Corinthians 1:27-31

5. In closing Paul repeats himself saying it is not about the works of the flesh (circumcision), but about the new creation – that only comes by faith in Jesus Christ. What will be the outcome of a life lived by grace (v. 16)?

How do the following Scriptures encourage and comfort you in your walk of grace?

a. John 16:33

b. Ephesians 2:4-9

Paul closes with a word marked by experience – the legalists would not embrace the cross because of the suffering that comes with following Jesus

– Paul says, "my body bears the scars of being a faithful follower." It was well worth it to him because of what Jesus had done for him at Calvary. How about you? Are you willing to whole-heartedly follow – no matter the consequences?

Verse 18 might be loosely translated – BROTHERS AND SISTERS, STICK WITH THE GRACE OF THE LORD JESUS CHRIST – THAT IS ALL YOU NEED!

6.   What specific lesson(s) did you learn from today's study and how will it make a difference in how you live this week?

7.   Continue to work on memorizing Galatians 6:7, 8 for this week.

DAY 6 – BEGIN IN PRAYER

1.   Read Galatians 6:1-18. (No Skipping – it's important!)

2.   How would you summarize the truths taught in verses 1-18?

3.   What truth has made a difference in your walk with the Lord this week?

4.   Can you record Galatians 6:7, 8 in the space below without looking at it? If not, continue to work on it today until you can.

"I HAVE BEEN CRUCIFIED WITH CHRIST; IT IS NO LONGER I WHO LIVE, BUT CHRIST LIVES IN ME; AND THE LIFE WHICH I NOW LIVE IN THE FLESH I LIVE BY FAITH IN THE SON OF GOD, WHO LOVED ME AND GAVE HIMSELF FOR ME."
                                                        GALATIANS 2:20

Morningstar
Inductive
Bible Studies

Morningstar Christian Chapel Inductive Bible Studies are designed to help believers go through the Bible and discover the rich truths of God's Word for themselves. Paul told Timothy to be a student of the Word (2 Timothy 2:15) and Peter encouraged us to have an answer for every man who asks for the hope that lies within us (1 Peter 3:15).

By breaking up each study into 6 days, with challenging questions and applications, the Inductive Study method will have you gleaning much from the awesome Word of God.

ISBN#	STUDY TITLE	LESSONS	MSRP
9780971573338	Abraham & Joseph	20	$20.00
9780972947725	Exodus	20	$20.00
9780972947732	Joshua	9	$13.00
9780972947787	King David	10	$13.00
9780971573314	John - Part 1	28	$24.00
9780971573376	John - Part 2	22	$24.00
9780971573321	Acts	27	$24.00
9780972947756	Galatians	12	$15.00
9780971573369	Ephesians	15	$15.00
9780971573345	Philippians	11	$13.00
9780971573352	Colossians	12	$15.00
9780971573307	James	20	$20.00
9780971573390	1 John	11	$13.00

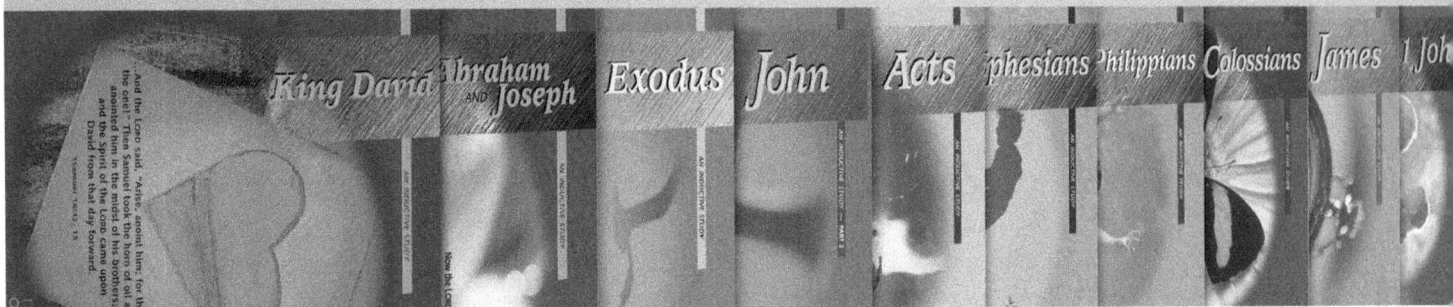

www.ingramcontent.com/pod-product-compliance
Lightning Source LLC
LaVergne TN
LVHW081346060426
835508LV00017B/1446